12/31/01

To:
Becky

From:
Beth

Happy New
Year 2002

*A friend loves at all times.*

Proverbs 17:17

May you have a
Happy Birthday and the
Lord brings you many
blessings this coming year!

# The Heart of a Lasting Friendship

Written and Illustrated by

## Audrey Jeanne Roberts

**■ Zondervan Publishing House**

*Grand Rapids, Michigan*
*A Division of* HarperCollins *Publishers*

*Dear Friend,*

I want to share a little peek into the journey that two of my lifelong friends and I made together. We'll travel from the surprise meetings that began our friendships, through the process of nurturing and developing those friendships. I'll also share how priceless a treasure our deep lasting friendships have become in our lives. Two very different people and uniquely different friends, Sally Dotson and Joan Fitzgerald have each played an important role in the Lord's ongoing process of shaping me into the person I am today.

If you had told me as a youngster, I would make my living as a writer and artist I'm sure I would have laughed endlessly! My formal art training consisted of one junior high art class. It was my deep desire to stay home and raise my children that started me searching for a way to earn the extra income our struggling family needed. In doing so I rediscovered one of my childhood joys...calligraphy. I never could have envisioned the course my life would take from there!

Joan and Sally recognized the tiniest seed of talent in

my early work, and encouraged it. They suggested I begin selling my work and even hosted home parties to start me off. Since the medium of calligraphy, by its very nature demands a message, I quickly discovered it wasn't easy to locate existing quotations or verse that captured the essence of the emotions, relationships and values I wanted to share with my customers.

At the same time, the Lord was teaching me things of lasting value through my friendships and in my every-day life as a wife and mother, and I was beginning to sense the call to share them.

I shared them through writing my own prose and poetry. I have been privileged to see my words touch hearts and change lives. My passion for words now far exceeds my passion for art.

Now come share a few moments with me as I tell you the story of how God gave me two lifelong friends who helped teach me how to be His friend. Let's journey together and find "The Heart of a Lasting Friendship."

Yours truly,

*Audrey Jeanne Roberts*

*Oak Haven Orchards*
*Valley Center, California*

To my precious friends,
Sally Dotson and Joan Fitzgerald
who have shared so much of this journey with me—
"thank you" seems such a paltry expression to convey how much
each of you means to me. You had the faith to see the tiniest seed
of talent and the fruitful tree God wanted to make out of it.  You
saw "the substance of things hoped for" and prayed it into reality.
Thank you from the bottom of my heart.

To my husband Stephen,
the love of my life—you give me the courage to attempt
the impossible. Your gift for words was a
special bonus I received when God gave you to me.
The Lord has used you to confirm His promises and direction
for my life from the day we met.
Thank you for being my very best friend.

Mostly, I thank the Lord
who promised me seventeen years ago that this day
would come and I, like Sarah, laughed.

*The LORD has done great things for us,*
*and we are filled with joy.*
Psalm 126:3

# Table of Contents

# Lifetime

Share their hopes and dreams,
Never worrying what
The other thinks.

Keep each other's confidences,
Providing a safe place
To reveal their deepest fears
And most heartfelt emotions.

Discover new insights and
Direction and are refreshed
And encouraged after they
Spend time together.

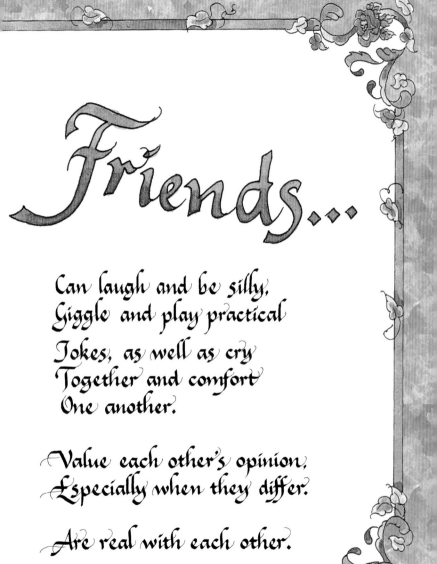

# Friends...

Can laugh and be silly,
Giggle and play practical
Jokes, as well as cry
Together and comfort
One another.

Value each other's opinion,
Especially when they differ.

Are real with each other.

# Building a lasting friendship means...

Not waiting 'til You have
time, But making Time for
each other. Doing little things
That matter...
  Short phone calls. A quick note,
And spontaneous visits
  Over coffee or tea.

Expressing your gratitude
And appreciation often,
Never assuming your friend
Knows how you Feel about her.

Listening as much as talking,
Always being open to advice
And wise counsel.
Holding your Counsel until asked,

Saying easily "I'm sorry" and
"You're forgiven."
Never taking your friendship
For granted, but seeing it
As one of God's special gifts.

Giving your relationship
The most precious of
All ingredients... Prayer and time...
Then sharing the matchless
Rewards of a

# Lifetime Friendship

*Audrey Jeanne Roberts*

# A Real Friend

I was still very young (just twenty-two), and our first child was well on her way. My husband, Jim, was not a believer at the time, and I had begun my own journey back to the Lord just before Jim and I were married three years ago. As is usually the case in unequally yoked marriages, ours had no shortage of difficulties and struggles. Adding to an already stressful situation, Jim was unemployed during the entire course of my pregnancy and didn't return to work until Jennifer was five months old. I was struggling to support the family with a fledgling art business. I knew that if I was to survive emotionally and spiritually in this difficult situation I desperately needed a real friend.

"Lord, please give me a real friend," was my heart's cry. "Someone who will challenge me to grow and draw closer to you. I'm so lonely. I need to be encouraged. I want to be needed. I need someone who knows my heart, who shares my values and my passion for you. I want to learn how to be a good friend as well. Please, God, give me someone who will become my best friend."

I waited, I watched, and I waited and watched some more. I pursued relationships only to have others not be as interested in friendship as I was—at least not at the same level that I wanted to relate. Not unlike a girl looking for a husband, I became consumed by my search for a special friend.

I was socially awkward and a "know it all"—a teacher in search of an audience! As I look back now, I can see that I was a most annoying creature. A few older women were praying for me, but I think they realized they didn't have the time to dedicate to my neediness and weren't called to *that* level of friendship with me. It seemed that no one stepped into the void in my life until the Lord knew I was *really* ready to have and be a special friend. Then he brought me Sally.

*"Lord, please give me a real friend"*

When Sally and I met, we were both hugely pregnant and attending the same small church. Before meeting her I heard over and over again, "You need to meet Sally." I guess everyone assumed we would automatically connect because we were both pregnant and due about the same time.

Belly-to-belly one day at church we introduced ourselves, just three weeks prior to my delivering Jennifer. I immediately thought, "Father, is this the friend I've been asking you for?" Though Sally and I talked a few times after that, there was some hesitation on her part to go deeper in our relationship.

Sally's son, Michael, was born two weeks after Jennifer. Sally's mother-in-law, Mimi, had been so certain her grandchild was going to be a girl that she had bought an extensive wardrobe of baby girl's clothing. Some she purchased new at Neiman-Marcus, some were garage sale finds, but none of her purchases were appropriate for her decidedly masculine-looking grandson!

The day Sally arrived home with Michael she called and asked me to come over. She knew that my husband had been out of work for more than a year and we couldn't afford to buy much for our new little daughter. When I arrived at her home, she gave me (with Mimi's permission) the entire wardrobe of beautiful girl's clothing.

I was overwhelmed. I was blessed. I was deeply touched. No gift could have meant more to me, except perhaps the gift of the budding friendship I thought we were sharing. However, all the while Sally was praying "Lord, if you don't want Audrey in my life, you can remove her! If you don't want her to be my friend, it's okay by me." She was already wrestling with my many irritating personality traits and wasn't sure she had the emotional energy a relationship with me would require.

*I was overwhelmed*

"Lord," she prayed, "surely you can't mean for us to be friends. We don't have a single thing in common except our love for you. She's ten years younger than I am and she thinks she knows everything!"

I was oblivious to the struggle Sally was having—though I'm sure she was sending out signals. I just kept going to her house, kept calling, and kept praying for a deep, special friendship. Finally, the Lord spoke to Sally during her quiet time one day. "You and Audrey are going to become like a weapon in my hands. I have forged your friendship as a weapon for me to use against the enemy and his kingdom of darkness. Are you willing to be used as that weapon?" Sally's heart melted and she prayed, "God, teach us how to be friends and give me a heart to love her exactly like she is. Give me your love for her, because mine isn't going to be enough."

Our long, wonderful friendship began the day Sally said "yes" to the Lord. Now when I think of realness in a friendship, Sally comes to mind as the perfect example. She has encouraged me and she has

*Sally's heart melted*

chastised me. She has given her counsel with wisdom and grace and has never pulled away from me when confrontation was needed.

Our friendship has not always gone smoothly. We've walked through difficulties. Though we are very different, God chose us to be friends for life, and he has been in this friendship. God knew we needed each other.

Real friends lay down their lives for you. They welcome you into their homes with open arms even though their houses may need to be cleaned. They are the first ones at your side in times of trauma and are the first to applaud your success. They pray for you and with you.

*Real friends are a gift from God, to be treasured always.*

*God* will meet all your needs
according to his glorious riches in
Christ Jesus.
*Philippians 4:19*

Be imitators of God as dearly loved
children and live a life of love, just as Christ
loved us and gave himself up for us as a
fragrant offering and sacrifice to God.
*Ephesians 5:1-2*

Be devoted to one another in brotherly love.
Honor one another above yourselves.
*Romans 12:10*

Share with God's people who are in need.
Practice hospitality.
*Romans 12:13*

# A Real Friend

A "real" friend doesn't hide the fact
that her fur is wearing thin.
She doesn't worry what I'll think
if her stuffing won't stay in.
She lets me see her any time,
on her shoulder I can cry.
And she'll use her favorite apron
to wipe my tears all dry.
No friend could ever be more true
she's as real as real can be...
Somehow, in spite of all my flaws
she likes the "real" me!

Audrey Jeanne Roberts

# Almost Instantly

I was twenty-four years old, my oldest daughter was two and a half and I was attending a women's Bible study at my church for the very first time. Because of our difficult financial situation and the long drive to church, my husband had not previously permitted me to attend. I was so excited to be going that I arrived quite early.

As little Jennifer and I walked across the parking lot, I looked up and observed a beautiful, elegant woman in a red silk dress get out of her car and begin walking in the same direction.

I looked down at my jeans and casual shirt thinking *Am I going to fit in? Am I dressed inappropriately? What kind of women will be attending?* I was self-conscious and self-absorbed, consumed by my own need to belong. Then I looked up just in time to see the woman trip. **She landed in my arms!** Her ankle gave way as she walked in high heels over the rough pavement, and she virtually landed in my arms!

Embarrassed, she introduced herself, "Hi, I'm Joan. Thanks for catching me!"

"I'm Audrey. Are you going to the women's Bible study?" I asked her.

"Yes. In fact, I'm teaching! You haven't been here before have you?" she noted. "Come with me and let me introduce you to everyone." With a warm smile and an enveloping hug, she both took me by the hand and tucked me under her wing.

Joan and I became friends that day and she loves to say, "I've been tripping and you've been catching me ever since!" The truth is we've both done our share of tripping into each other's arms.

Our friendship was virtually instant. Communication has been almost unnecessary at times as we seem to sense each other's needs. There is a spiritual camaraderie between us; we both hungered for the Lord and his best in our lives and we long to be used for any purpose he has in mind. In a very short time it seemed as though we had known each other forever, and we almost couldn't remember life before we met!

*Our friendship was virtually instant*

Becoming instant friends and soul mates—how can you explain it? The one-heartedness is beyond words. Whether you and your friend are similar in nature or as different as night and day, you just know you were meant to be friends forever. It seems you never run out of things to talk about, and the time you share flies by much too quickly. You enjoy learning more and more about each other—likes, dislikes, needs, dreams, passions—and the other relationships in your lives.

Even when weeks fly past and the circumstances of life don't allow the luxury of long, intimate times together, you can pick up the phone and start where you left off, whether you last talked two weeks ago or two months ago.

This kind of friendship is a precious gift from God. Sometimes it's *Friendship is a precious gift* easier to recognize the gift because of the amazing circumstances that may have brought you together. Yesterday you had never met; today you're well on your way to becoming best friends!

# No eye has seen,

no ear has heard,
no mind has conceived what God has prepared
for those who love him.
*1 Corinthians 2:9*

Every good and perfect gift is from above,
coming down from the Father of the heavenly lights.
*James 1:17*

Come and see what God has done, how awesome
his works in man's behalf!
*Psalm 66:5*

The LORD longs to be gracious to you;
he rises to show you compassion.
*Isaiah 30:18*

Almost
Instantly...

As if we'd known
each other forever
We were the

Deepest
of
friends

Never lacking
things to say or
Thoughts to share.

# Nearly Timeless

Even when weeks fly by and we
Struggle to stay in touch
All it takes is a moment and
Our hearts are brought together
again...

# Almost Instantly

*Audrey Jeanne Roberts*

# Weaving Our Lives Together

It requires two kinds of threads to create a weaving, the warp and the woof. Warp and woof go in completely opposite directions and are often of entirely different materials. The two balls of thread or other material, before being woven, have little or no purpose. But when woven together upon the loom by the master weaver, the manner in which the two interact produces the pattern of the weave and together the threads produce a fabric that has both beauty and usefulness. They become fit for the purpose for which the weaver has paired them.

Sometimes the weaving process can be a little uncomfortable, requiring stretching, compromise, and flexibility. Our friendships are like the threads on the loom. We're pulled this way or that. We're stretched and crossed over each other, and then packed tightly together to form an entirely unique fabric. But the result is more than worth the discomfort of the process.

Sally and I are so different it is comical. On one of our shopping trips I pulled a lovely, muted floral dress off the rack and held it up for her to view. "Ugh! That looks like something my grandmother would wear!" she exclaimed. "You don't really like that, do you?" Later in our favorite fabric shop she draped an orange-red, Indian sari cloth with gold metallic highlights around her neck. "I can't believe you would even consider wearing something that gaudy!" was my reaction.

Sally and I see life from different vantage points. In our early years this led to frustration and confusion in our communication. If we were looking at a situation in our lives like it were a mountain, I might describe it like this, "The mountain is steep with dangerous trails and rock faces, it will take a week to climb with full mountain gear." Sally would say, "No it's *Our friendships are like threads* not. It has a gently winding path leading up to the top. I could walk it in a day in tennis shoes." Who was right and who was wrong? We discovered that neither of us was entirely correct. We were simply standing on different sides of the same mountain! We realized that only God from his vantage point could take in the whole view at one time. He had, however, given us to each other so that with our different viewpoints, we might see more of the mountain than either of us could see alone. We each perceived truths that could be of assistance to the other, and we learned to value our differences and listen to each other's counsel.

When we pray together, Sally often thinks of things to pray that would never have entered my mind. She sometimes sees the answer when I'm unable to see past the problem. When I encounter difficulties in parenting and turn to her for advice, I never cease to be amazed at the wisdom she has to offer me. Because she is older than I am and has parented through more stages than I, her experience as well as her differences help me to see the problem just like that mountain—from all sides. Then I can select the simplest and easiest route to the top.

As God weaves people and their differences together to create a beautiful pattern, he also weaves circumstances into their lives to further enhance their strength and beauty. The skillful weaver understands that he must sometimes mix a deep black or dull gray thread into the pattern in order to gain the greatest beauty. Without the dark threads, the light threads will only seem pale and washed out. But the contrast between the lightest hues and the deepest darks adds richness and highlights the beauty of the lighter threads.

So it is in our lives. How often we wish that life could be woven together of only light, bright hues. How wonderful that would be! But in reality it is in the dark times, in the seasons of difficulty, that we come to value and fully treasure our friendships, because those times add richness, and depth to our lives and highlight the beauty of the bright, joyful days. A friend who sticks by your side when all others are leaving, who speaks words of encouragement and hope when others are condemning or discouraging is the friend you value. That friend sparkles in the darkness. When you have come through the dark times together, you find your hearts are even more closely woven together than you ever thought they could be, and the joys you share are doubled in intensity. When you allow your lives to be woven together through good times

*The joys you share are doubled*

and tough times, you allow God to create a pattern of beauty uniquely and wonderfully your own. Let God weave your lives together.

*Lord*, weave our lives together and make of them

a thing of beauty and usefulness.

*Audrey Jeanne Roberts*

# O Lord,

You are our Father. We are the clay,
you are the potter; we are all the work of your hand.
*Isaiah 64:8*

It is God who works in you to will and to act
according to his good purpose.
*Philippians 2:13*

In Christ you are being built together to become
a dwelling in which God lives by his Spirit.
*Ephesians 2:22*

Glorify the LORD with me; let us
exalt his name together.
*Psalm 34:3*

# Friendship

is like a tapestry that has
been woven of many
vibrant hues.

It is created with the
finest shimmering threads,
strategically placed against
a field of darks.

Then each knot is skillfully
fastened with patience and
tender care.

Its value, like the finest
art, increases steadily with
the passage of time.

Your friendship

has become my treasure

Audrey Jeanne Roberts

# The Seasons
## of a Friendship

When Sally and I had babies at the same time, we constantly lamented about our exhaustion and lack of sleep. We were both surprised by the intense requirements of parenting babies and toddlers. Even though we were so overwhelmingly busy, we somehow found time to go to the park with the children and took time to talk every single day. We also found we could talk and pray as we cleaned our houses or prepared dinner.

One of the older women in a Bible study I taught at the time cautioned us, "If you think you're busy now, wait until you get into your forties and your children are teenagers. You won't believe how much you are capable of doing or will be required to do. Your teenagers will need you even more than your toddlers."

At the time we thought, *She's just forgotten what it's like having babies. Nothing could be tougher than this!* But now that we are "forty-something," we've learned how very right she was.

*We need prayer more now*

One of the dangers of the increasing load of responsibility of the middle years is that friendships may be put on hold or fall by the wayside. Our afternoons of prayer now seem like a luxury. I think it is quite possible that we need prayer more now than ever before, yet our lives have crowded that time out.

The middle years seem to put us in the middle of meeting a number of needs; our children's and husband's (if we're married), our work, our church, and often our aging parents' needs as well. Those who face the daunting task of single parenting have double the load with no relief to spell them. There is very little time or energy left for us, and we feel guilty if we even think of letting someone else's needs go unmet while we take time to meet our own. The result is that we have very little time left for friendship.

But don't shortchange yourself. Make the effort, create the time and space for your friend. You will value the objective sounding board that you can be to each other. Your friendship might be one of the only safe, neutral places you have to unload your frustrations and concerns.

*Don't shortchange yourself.*

Friendship takes time and energy. Sometimes we feel it is time and energy we can't spare. Yet often it is the time spent with a friend that recharges us to go back into the battle with renewed hope and perspective. Isn't it true that the time we spend praying with each other brings the answer to our trials? Can we afford NOT to take time for friendship?

Friendships will change with the seasons of our lives.

When we are young and unmarried, we can spend every Friday or Saturday night out with "the gang" or with a special friend. When we marry we have new responsibilities. Then when we become parents, even more responsibilities interject themselves between us and our friends. Though we sometimes long for the early days, life marches on.

When our children become teenagers and are heading to young adulthood, our greatest stresses and challenges may develop. During this time we need a friend more than ever to help us hold on to our sanity and sense of humor. Perhaps a friend will need to remind us that we'll never have the joys of grandparenthood if we strangle our children!

Then come the empty nest years and a friendship that has endured can become a great blessing to our empty hearts and homes. If throughout the years we have stayed in touch and continued to let our friendship grow, we may once

*Friendships will change*

again find that sweet, leisurely companionship when our children have gone. Once again there may be time to play, to pray, and to enjoy each other's company in a precious new way. But those rewards will only come if we keep growing in friendship through the seasons of life.

# Lord,

Help us to maintain the closeness
of our early years through all that life
will bring our way. Remind us how important
our times of sharing, caring and praying for
each other are and show us creative ways to
make our time together really count.
We need to be reminded often how precious
and important this gift of friendship is.
It's like a beautiful garden…
help us to tend it faithfully so we can enjoy
its bounty for a lifetime.

# Let us not

give up meeting together, as some
are in the habit of doing,
but let us encourage one another.
*Hebrews 10:25*

Perfume and incense bring joy
to the heart, and the pleasantness
of one's friend springs from his
earnest counsel.
*Proverbs 27:9*

There is a time for everything,
and a season for every activity
under heaven...
God has made everything beautiful
in its time.
*Ecclesiastes 3:1,11*

Above all,
love each other deeply.
*1 Peter 4:8*

Pursue righteousness, faith, love
and peace, along with those who
call on the Lord out of a pure heart.
*2 Timothy 2:22*

I thank my God every time
I remember you. In all my prayers
for all of you, I always pray with joy.
*Philippians 1:3-4*

In everything,
do to others what you would have
them do to you.
*Matthew 7:12*

The seasons in our lives
Have come and gone.
In misty remembrance
For old days we long.

# Lasting

As youths we had time
To share from our hearts,
But now we're always
Playing our part.

Being a wife and a mother
Leave less time you see.
But you're always there,
Friends we'll always be.

## Friendships

For in time this season
Too will pass
Leaving you and me
And a friendship that lasts.

*Audrey Jeanne Roberts*

# A Friendship That Goes the Distance

Friendship with Sally used to be easy. We lived less than a mile apart and could see each other virtually at will. Many were the days when she would come home from the grocery store, drive down my street, and drop in for chat and a cup of tea.

This past week, after writing most of this chapter, I called her to talk about the book. Before I had even shared my thoughts with her, she reminded me of an afternoon we spent at the park when our children were young.

It was a perfect, Southern California spring day. The sun was warm and inviting. The temperature was mild, the breeze gently stirring. We fixed peanut butter and jelly sandwiches and threw a few other odds and ends together for lunch and headed to our neighborhood park. After eating, we sat on a gentle, grassy slope overlooking the kids playing on the swing set.

Sally recalled, "You looked up at the sky, the trees, the flowers and then at me and said 'I'm going to remember this day... this is so special and so wonderful. I'm going to ask God to help me file it away in my memory so that it will always be there to treasure.'"

"Audrey, you taught me a lesson that day," Sally related, "and I've never forgotten it. Memories can be created at will by the thankful heart. When I am appreciative of the moment and take time to meditate on it, it becomes a sweet memory I can treasure forever!"

I also remembered that afternoon. I knew how much we valued those times. But the question kept circling in my mind, "How much more would we have valued them if we knew one day we would no longer have the luxury of living near each other?"

But even before I moved 40 miles away, it had become increasingly difficult to stay connected. We had to work harder and plan ahead more. My business and career grew exponentially in the ensuing years. Sally went back to work as a nurse. My second marriage and newly blended family *"I'm going to remember this day"* required time and attention to grow. Where was that luxurious thing we once enjoyed—"time to spare?" Sally and I are realizing that we could lose the very special gift that God has given to us if we don't nurture it with the life-sustaining ingredient of time.

I've talked with many people about their friendships. Most feel that they don't have enough time to spend with their friends. Life is overloaded with schedules. Work has expanded. Children's activities keep parents tied up as well. We feel that something has to give. More often than not, that something is friendship.

How can we maintain friendships that have become distanced, whether by time or loca- *How can* tion? How can we experience the *we maintain* closeness and bonding that we *friendships?* had in our early years throughout the lifetime of our friendship? Here are some simple, practical steps that will help your friendship thrive.

*The first thing to do is pray.* Ask God to give you unique ideas that will help you maintain your friendship. He can multiply the effectiveness of your time together. Some of my most delightful memories are of spontaneous, God-inspired outings with my buddies.

*Don't expect to find time—make time.* It doesn't require large segments of time to stay connected. Make short visits. Share tasks like shopping or doing necessary errands together. Make short but frequent phone calls. Send a quick email if you have internet access. Ask questions that show you care, communicate your love, or share a joke you heard today.

*Ask God to remind you to call or to pray.* Each time he brings your friend to mind, ask him what you should pray. You'll be amazed at what he'll bring to mind and how wonderfully he'll keep you connected. Each of these prayers is like a little string that links our hearts together as one.

*Try to plan a get-together or other special time once or twice a year.* It doesn't have to cost much or be elaborate. Just being together for the day can bring refreshment to your souls! Go to a retreat together, be roommates and talk into the wee hours of the morning, then plan a power nap for the next afternoon to recover!

*At the beginning of the year, write reminders in your daily planner to call your friend each week.* Even if you don't call each week, you'll call more often if you write it on your calendar.

*Pick up small, special gifts for no occasion at all*—the kind of gifts that remind your friend how much you care and that you are thinking about her. Or drop a simple note in the mail. There's nothing like *Remind your friend you care* a note to make you feel loved and special. I have a friendship with a fellow artist, Mara. We've formed a two-woman "artist's support group," and it's wonderful to be able to talk with someone who knows the pressure of deadlines as well as the dual curses of all artists, perfectionism and procrastination.

Mara often sends me encouraging little notes written right on a magazine article she thought I would be interested in or on a card she created with her own hands. It means so much to me that she took a moment out of her busy day to send me something I might need to know.

If writing is not an area you're comfortable with, remember that short meaningful notes sent frequently will mean a lot more than an epic communication sent once a year. Your friend will not be editing your note. She'll treasure it as an expression of your love for her.

*Don't forget to share your needs with your friend.* It seems that the farther apart we grow in time or distance, the easier it is to forget to be real. Real friendship is about taking turns helping each other. It's about sharing your fears and concerns as well as the most eventful things in your lives. Ask your friend often, "What's the hardest thing you're going through right now and what can I do to be of help

*Real friendship is helping each other*

to you? What can I pray about?" Ask your friend to share dreams and goals with you and commit yourself to pray for those goals to be accomplished.

There is no distance in the spirit or in the heart, once friends' hearts have been joined as one. All it takes is a little maintenance to continue reaping a lifetime of blessings.

Roberts
le Rd.
CA
92082

**Addresses**

Susan Arden 415-555-4702
P O Box 1981
San Francisco, CA

Grandma Alice

4769 Carriage Rd.

Lancaster, PA

Susan Arden
P.O. Box 1981
San Francisco

Susan! It's so hard
to draw by your old house &
know you're not there anymore.
How's life in the big city?
Have you been to any museums
yet? There are so many wonderful
ones there. Did you know there's
a Monet Waterlily land at one of
them? You have to see it... it's so

## May the Lord

keep watch between you
and me when we are away
from each other.
*Genesis 31:49*

Let us consider how we
may spur one another on toward
love and good deeds.
*Hebrews 10:24*

Do not forget to do good
and to share with others,
for with such sacrifices God is pleased.
*Hebrews 13:16*

Be kind and compassionate
to one another.
*Ephesians 4:32*

Live in harmony with
one another;
be sympathetic, love,...
be compassionate and humble.
*1 Peter 3:8*

Keep on loving each other.
*Hebrews 13:1*

Encourage one another daily.
*Hebrews 3:13*

# My Faraway Friend

Once we lived so close...it took no effort to see you. Now the miles stretch out between us and so many times I think, I'll drop over, only to realize, I can't.

The wonderful thing is there is no time or distance between our hearts! The moment we talk, we pick up right where we left off days or weeks ago. You know me so well you always know just what to say, you know when I'm down, when I'm serious or when I'm teasing.

I wish we lived closer, but

## I'm so glad our hearts will always be close.

Audrey Jeanne Roberts

*Audrey Brennan* ©1990

# I Knew You When...

There is something so special and fun about long-lasting friendships. Perhaps you have a friend you've known since long before you were married, had children, got pudgy, turned gray, or got wrinkled! You may remember your friend's "raw material," and now you have the joy of seeing her become all that God wants her to be.

When people meet me now, they always assume I planned to be a writer, speaker,  and artist. They assume I took art classes and studied speech and literature in college. Only my best friends know the strange and crooked path the Lord led me on to bring me to this place in my life. They have watched me struggle to find God's will and direction. They've prayed with me as I submitted my will, my desires, my dreams, and asked him to give me his will, his desires, and his dreams for my life.

*They have watched me struggle*

People who meet me now see a fairly confident, poised woman, comfortable with speaking in public or meeting just about anyone, anywhere. But my best friends remember praying with me before those first speaking engagements long ago, when I was so nervous I couldn't eat. They remember that I talked so fast no one could follow me, that I forgot half of what I had planned to say, and that I said things that didn't even make sense! At the time my stumbling speech was embarrassing, but now those memories aren't painful any longer. In fact, they are a priceless treasure because they remind me of how much my friends have built me up and helped me grow.

Now my friends and I laugh with joy at the foibles and foolishness of our early years. We laugh at how fearful we were to trust God then, making decisions and commitments with great difficulty and anguish. Now we can make them without struggle as we've learned the joy of living life God's way. We laugh at how *Lifelong friends* overwhelming situations *know your* became incredibly wonderful victories. We rejoice over seeing *weaknesses* a thousand different prayers for our children answered right before our very eyes.

Lifelong friends also give you a reliable perspective. It's easy for me to say to Sally, "God will provide finances for your son's Christian school this year." I've already seen God miraculously provide every year for nineteen years! And it's easy for her to say, "God will give you the words and the inspiration for the designs you need to get done," because she's seen me struggle, pray, and worry that I won't meet a deadline, and she's seen God give me ideas or designs I could never have thought of on my own.

Lifelong friends know your weaknesses, too. They know when you're not really giving your full effort, or when you're making excuses, and they love you enough to challenge you to do your best. They know the areas where your faith is weak, and they point you back to the Lord rather than bail you out. They can see when you are slipping into doubt, depression, or unbelief, and they are right there to pick you up and dust you off when you fall down. There is something especially comforting about a friend who has walked with you through an entire lifetime. My editor, Gwen Ellis, recently experienced the death of her father. When it happened, all she had to do was to call her childhood friend, Merle Ann. Though Merle Ann was in another city an hour away, the first words out of her mouth were, "I'm coming, I'll be there." There is great reward in investing in a lifetime of friendship.

# *He who walks*

with the wise grows wise.
*Proverbs 13:20*

As iron sharpens iron,
so one...sharpens another.
*Proverbs 27:17*

Wounds from a friend can be trusted.
*Proverbs 27:6*

A man of many companions
may come to ruin, but there is a friend
who sticks closer than a brother.
*Proverbs 18:24*

# Lifelong Friendship

From the earliest days
of our friendship,
we knew it would last a lifetime.
We've walked many different
roads together.
At times you've held me up
other times, you've had
to lean upon me.
Most of the time,
we've just enjoyed the view
side by side.
What a joy, sharing so many
of life's most memorable moments
with someone

## As special as you!

*Audrey Jeanne Roberts*

# Someone to Lean On

When my first husband, Jim was diagnosed with cancer, I was asked this question: "What has been the best preparation to help you walk through this trial?" I had to think for a few moments before I responded. "First, I'm most thankful for every other trial I have faced because through them I have learned that God is absolutely trustworthy. Even if the worst happens, God will be more than enough for me. Secondly, I'm so thankful that I have been deeply planted in a church body and have established friendships all around me. I don't have any time to develop them now in the swirling, overwhelming chaos of this crisis."

In times of trouble a good friend just might be your only visible means of support. Like the life ring thrown to someone who is drowning, a friend can help you hold your head above the water *A precious friend can help you* until your rescuer comes. Only God can rescue you, but a precious friend can help you to hold on to your hope, your courage, and your faith.

If you asked each of my friends whether they had done enough to help me when Jim was dying, they would answer in unison, "No. I could have done more. I should have done more." They would feel that what they did was too small and inconsequential. But I don't feel that way. Each one gave me a priceless gift: prayers, phone calls, meals, childcare. Just small and ordinary things, but like priceless jewels they were of immense and incalculable value to me.

How can you be a friend to someone in difficult circumstances? It is really very simple. *Do the little things.* Show Christ's love by attending to the ordinary. Help with the laundry, go shopping, care for the children, or just hold your friend and let her cry. In times *"I've been* of trouble, we as friends feel so inade- *praying..."* quate. We ask ourselves, "What if I say the wrong thing? What if I do the wrong thing? What if it's not enough?" Let me encourage you. It's the ordinary, small things done with a heart of love and concern that will mean the most.

What meant the most to me was Eunice bringing me a meal of tofu lasagna once a week. It was receiving phone calls from people in my Bible study group who started the conversation with, "The Lord put you on my heart today and I've been praying..." and then went on to tell me very specific prayers that they had prayed for me. It wasn't just, "I'll pray for you," but proof that they had already prayed for me.

In the midst of a trial there is joy and solace in having

friends who already know your heart and who have good insights into your struggles, emotionally, spiritually, and relationally. My grieving process was complicated by many factors. I had prayed for Jim's salvation and for a good marriage for sixteen years. My friends understood the bittersweet emotions I was experiencing as I watched my longtime prayers being answered before my eyes at the cost of my husband's physical life. They understood my incredible joy in watching him yield his heart to the Lord just months before his death, and my grief at then losing him and any chance of having the relationship for which I had yearned.

*Good friends give you perspective*

Good friends help remind you of God's promises when life seems dark and out of control. Good friends intercept you on the way to your pity party and remind you of all that is good in your life and worth living for. Good friends give you perspective, because they can see beyond what you are capable of seeing at the moment. Good friends touch you. They hold your hand. They pat you on the back or give you a big hug just when you need it most. Medical research has shown that people with good friends live longer and are healthier and happier and these are just some of the reasons why. Often, one of the first questions asked when a diagnosis of serious illness is given is,

"What kind of support network do you have?"

In real life, when a crisis comes, you won't have time to develop friendships. Develop your friendships now. Invest in each other's lives now. Don't wait until you "have time."

Make time for friendships; they just might save your life!

# Carry

each other's burdens, and in this way
you will fulfill the law of Christ.
*Galatians 6:2*

As we have opportunity, let us do good
to all people, especially to those who belong
to the family of believers.
*Galatians 6:10*

Rejoice with those who rejoice;
mourn with those who mourn.
*Romans 12:15*

An anxious heart weighs a man down,
but a kind word cheers him up.
*Proverbs 12:25*

Your sun will never set again,
and your moon will wane no more;
the LORD will be your everlasting light,
and your days of sorrow will end.
*Isaiah 60:20*

"I will turn their mourning into gladness;
I will give them comfort and joy instead of sorrow,"
declares the LORD.
*Jeremiah 31:13*

Let us approach the throne of grace
with confidence, so that we may receive mercy
and find grace to help us in our time of need.
*Hebrews 4:16*

My intercessor is my friend
as my eyes pour out tears to God.
*Job 16:20*

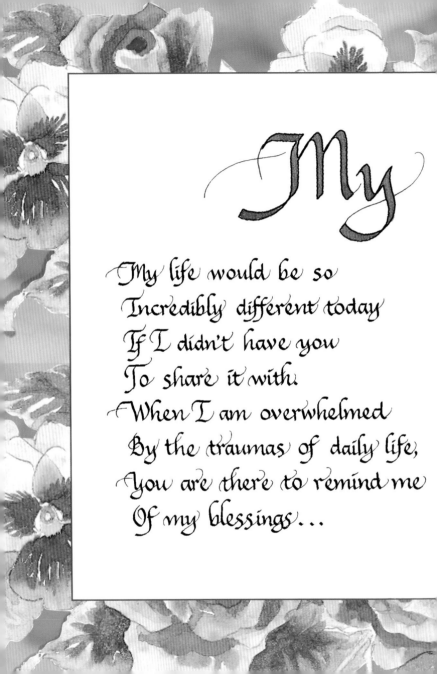

# My

My life would be so
Incredibly different today
If I didn't have you
To share it with.
When I am overwhelmed
By the traumas of daily life,
You are there to remind me
Of my blessings…

# Friend

Large and small.
You listen carefully, see clearly
And help me put things into
Perspective. I know I am a
Better person since you
Became a

## part of my life!

*Audrey Jeanne Roberts*

# Friends Are Family We Choose For Ourselves

Families were designed by God to be a blessing. A strong, healthy family brings a joy that nothing in life can surpass. But not all of us are fortunate enough to have been raised in a healthy, happy family. What can you do if you can't communicate your spiritual values with those who share a blood connection with you? How can you fill the deep need of your heart to belong in a family?

God made friendships to help fill the empty places in our lives. If you always wanted a sister but never had one, God may give you a sister of the heart instead. Though you didn't grow **Friendships fill the empty places** up in the same household, you won't be able to imagine how you could be any closer even if you had! If your mother has passed away, or perhaps simply has never been able to meet your emotional needs, God may give you an older woman to mentor you and share both her wisdom and her love with you.

This past summer, I attended Sally's son Michael's high school graduation party at Sally's house. I found myself looking around at each of the familiar faces that were present, and the memories of the past flooded my mind. Sally and I have shared so much of life that she has become in every way my "other sister." I hardly think of her as just a friend anymore. I've also been included in birthday parties, holiday celebrations, weddings, and graduations with her family. Her family has in many ways become my family as well.

Joan's family has out and out adopted me! We have prayed through court cases, battles with cancer, untimely deaths, and traumatic accidents. One court case lasted for years and was only resolved through the family's continuous, intense intercession. I've

*Joan's family has adopted me*

been privileged to walk through the trials and share the victories of life with them.

Both of these families prayed for us when Jim's cancer was first diagnosed. They stood with us through his terminal illness and upheld me when I was left widowed at the age of thirty-five with two small children. Later when I was blessed to meet my husband, Stephen, and began a new life, my "family" was there to check him out and receive him into their families as well.

After Joan's father, Claude, passed away in 1997, I found out he had emotionally adopted me as his fourth daughter. I never knew it at the time, but he had prayed for me every day just like he prayed for his own children. He had written about me in his journal and though he never said it in life, his words were left behind for me so that I could know how much he considered me a part of their family.

Good friendships can help us to fill in the gaps in current family relationships. Good friends can become the family we never had or the one we always longed for. Friends are family we choose for ourselves!

There is a friend that sticks closer than a brother
Proverbs 18:24

*God* chose us in him
before the creation of the world to be holy
and blameless in his sight. In love he predestined us
to be adopted as his sons through Jesus Christ,
in accordance with his pleasure and will—
to the praise of his glorious grace,
which he has freely given us in the One he loves.
*Ephesians 1:4-6*

How great is the love the Father has
lavished on us, that we should be called
children of God! And that is what we are!
*1 John 3:1*

Let the peace of Christ rule
in your hearts, since as members of one body
you were called to peace.
*Colossians 3:15*

To be

We've shared
so much laughter,
Shared so many tears,
We've a spiritual kinship
That grows stronger each year.
We're not sisters by birth
But we knew from the start
God put us together

sisters by heart

# One Plus One is Greater Than Two

This evening, my family and I attended a performance of "The Nutcracker Suite" put on by the Moscow Ballet. It was spectacularly beautiful. I was absolutely mesmerized by the sets, the costumes, and the athletic beauty of the dance itself.

As the story unfolded, I noticed the prince's supportive role to Clara. Every move he made, every lift, and every spin was designed to make her shine. There was a wonderful selflessness evidenced in their partnership. For the play to sparkle, his role was to make sure she was highlighted. She was lifted up, she was the focus of all eyes, but it was he who held her in his strong arms.

*She was the focus of all eyes*

Towards the close of this performance, the prince and Clara danced separately. Each was an incredible performer. His jumps were astoundingly executed and he danced powerfully and gracefully. I was amazed at his skill. She took her turn, dancing flawlessly on point, spinning with speed, balance, and precision. Her elegance and beauty was a match for the timeless role. I realized what remarkable athletes each were separately.

I also realized that the prince had held back from showcasing his own skill to fulfill the role he was cast in, and that as strong as they each were individually, when brought together, Clara and the prince became greater than the sum of their individual parts.

This ballet partnership is a parallel of friendship. Each individual must be strong. Each must be whole and complete on her own. Yet when they are brought into each other's lives, they can become greater together than either could be on her own. God uses us to augment and complete one another. Sometimes one friend will shine brighter than the other. But what is important is that we play the role God has called us to play.

*Sometimes one friend will shine brighter*

Some years ago, my friend Joan had a weekend speaking engagement at a women's retreat in San Mateo, California, and she invited me along to help her out. It was such a joy to stand in the back of the room praying for her and for the women that attended. No one noticed I was there, but I didn't care. It was Joan's turn to shine. God gave me such joy and satisfaction in the quiet and hidden role he had called me to play. It wasn't my season to be in front, I wasn't ready or prepared, nor did I have any desire to be in the spotlight. And Joan was blessed because she knew she was fulfilling her role in a more effective manner because I was there praying for her.

Friends lend each other strength. They pick each other up when they fall and lift each other high. Friends serve one another from a heart of love without thought of being honored or rewarded. Friends rejoice in the accomplishments of one another without jealousy or competition. Joy in a triumph or victory is only made complete when shared with a friend.

Most friendships will go through seasons of shifting roles. Sometimes you will be in the spotlight and friends will be in the supporting roles. At other times it will be the reverse. In my friendship with Joan, our roles

*Friends lend each other strength*

have changed, and I now find myself unexpectedly in the "up front" position. I'll bet you can guess where Joan is right now—joyfully praying in the background for God to bless me and for his purposes to be served.

# Two

are better than one,
because they have a good return
for their work:
If one falls down, his friend
can help him up.
But pity the man who falls
and has no one to help him up!
Also, if two lie down together,
they will keep warm.
But how can one keep warm alone?
Though one may be overpowered,
two can defend themselves.
A cord of three strands
is not quickly broken.
*Ecclesiastes 4:9-12*

# Lord,

Show me ways I can help
my friend to "shine." Show me
how to encourage her,
lift her up and be supportive
in every way I can.
Help me to have a servant's heart,
to serve her and not need
to be noticed or rewarded.
Make the two of us
greater together
than either could be alone!

A true friend is one
who ignores your
broken down gate and
admires your garden

# My Heart is One With Yours

"After David had finished talking with Saul, Jonathan became one in spirit with David, and he loved him as himself. ... And Jonathan made a covenant with David because he loved him as himself. Jonathan took off the robe he was wearing and gave it to David, along with his tunic and even his sword, his bow and his belt" (1 Samuel 18:1, 3-4).

Jonathan is one of my heroes. He is the son of the king, heir apparent to the throne of Israel, yet Jonathan hungers only for one thing—the will of God in his life. David was just a shepherd boy the day Jonathan met him. He was still young and from an entirely different social circle and status in life. But Jonathan put aside those exterior differences and looked (as God did) upon David's heart. Jonathan recognized in David the same uncompromising, fearless faith in the living God of Israel that Jonathan himself had demonstrated when just he *David was a shepherd boy* and his armor bearer took on twenty Philistine warriors. Their courage empowered by God incited a panic that ultimately routed the entire Philistine army.

David and Jonathan probably had very little in common. Jonathan was the "king's kid" and first in line for the throne. His days were filled with courtly duties and leadership. David was the youngest of eight sons. He spent his days tending sheep, playing music, and worshiping the Lord alone in the hills. What David and Jonathan had in common was found in the deepest recesses of their hearts.

They shared a radical faith in the God of Israel to always deliver. Both understood the greatness of their God and his ability to

**They shared a radical faith**

use any man, great or small, to accomplish his purposes. As a result, each became a mighty warrior for God.

When Jonathan heard David tell Saul his story of killing Goliath, Jonathan saw that David wasn't exalting himself. He was exalting God, their deliverer. It was this humble, godly heart that Jonathan loved, and in a single hour his heart was knit together with David's for all eternity.

Jonathan and David's friendship was powerful. It was instant. It was lasting. Their covenant of friendship and the story of their love has been a blessing to every generation since.

Jonathan cared for the people and he cared for God. He would have been just as happy serving David. Unlike his father, he wasn't threatened by David's exploits or his reputation. Jonathan was happy to take a back seat and to let David shine. At their last recorded meeting, Jonathan committed himself to God's will and to David, even above his commitment to his father. "Don't be afraid," he said. "My father Saul will not lay a hand on you. You will be king over Israel, and I will be second to you. Even my father Saul knows this" (1 Samuel 23:17).

Sally and I are as different as David and Jonathan. On the surface there was so little to recommend us as friends. But God knew our hearts and he knew the plans he had for us! When we were able to look past our very different exterior packages and see into each other's hearts, we became one in spirit and loved each other as ourselves. It doesn't matter how many differences there may be between you and your friend. Perhaps you have distinctly different personalities, or are quite far apart in age. You may have a different marital status, or career, or be at different stations in life than your friend. But the true power of friendship is released when you look past the exterior and become one in heart and soul.

*God knew our hearts*

God loves it when we have the same humble attitude in our friendships that Christ Jesus had. He wants us to be "like-minded, having the same love, being one in spirit and purpose. Do nothing out of selfish ambition or vain conceit, but in humility consider others better than yourselves. Each of you should look not only to your own interests, but also to the interests of others" (Philippians 2:2-4).

When we share a love for God and his people, when we selflessly lay down our lives for each other, considering each other more highly than ourselves, God is pleased. He loves to shine through us and through our friendships. He will bless your friendship in ways you cannot begin to comprehend. Perhaps your love will even shine like Jonathan and David's for many generations!

*God will bless your friendship*

*My precious friend, I bear in mind.
That faithful friends are hard to find.
In you I've found one good and true.
And yearly grows my love for you.*

Adapted from Victorian Verse

# *Jonathan said to David,*

"We have sworn friendship with each other
in the name of the LORD, saying,
'The LORD is witness between you and me,
and between your descendants and
my descendants forever.'"
*1 Samuel 20:42*

Make every effort to keep
the unity of the Spirit through the bond of peace.
*Ephesians 4:3*

May the God who gives endurance
and encouragement give you a spirit of unity
among yourselves as you follow Christ Jesus,
so that with one heart and mouth you may glorify
the God and Father of our Lord Jesus Christ.
*Romans 15:5-6*

# Dear friends,

let us love one another,
for love comes from God. Everyone
who loves has been born
of God and knows God.
*1 John 4:7*

Jesus prayed, "Holy Father, protect
[those you have given me]
by the power of your name—
the name you gave me—
so that they may be one
as we are one."
*John 17:11*

Follow the way of love.
*1 Corinthians 14:1*

People are like
stained glass windows.
They glow & sparkle when
it's sunny and bright;
but when the sun goes
down their true beauty
is revealed only if
there is a light
from within

Author Unknown

# Friends in the Workplace

Finding friends in the workplace can be difficult. When I was first married I worked for a worker's compensation insurance company. It was such a dismal emotional environment that I dreaded going to work each morning. There was backbiting, gossip, and internal power struggles. At break time, I hated going into the lunchroom. A large number of women who worked in and around my department were divorced. They had become angry, bitter, and disgusted with men and life in general. Sitting through a lunch with them meant hearing negative, cynical, and often coarse discussions about the nature of men.

It was such a temptation to join the complaining because they would have supported me. "Oh you poor girl. He's treating you wrong. You deserve better. Dump him, you can find someone better. You deserve someone better." Fortunately, I was wise enough to realize that while it would feel good to be "encouraged" *I would have grown hardhearted* by their foolish advice, it would lead to devastation in my home life. If I'd fallen into the trap of discussing the latest wound my husband had inflicted, I would have grown hardhearted and bitter toward him. Their advice wasn't given with my best interest at heart, but only as a way to vent their own opinions. They didn't really care about my marriage and they didn't want to help me work through my difficulties.

I prayed, "Lord help me to find someone at this company who will encourage me to grow in you. Someone who will help me to do what's right and will be an encouraging voice in this vast sea of negativity." I waited, but as far as I was aware, there wasn't another Christian on my entire floor. Some time passed and the company hired a new typist. Bernice

*What a difference her presence made*

sat directly across from me. The Lord put her on my heart and I began to befriend her. She was a young single mother who was struggling with hard questions and great needs.

After a time, I had the privilege of leading her back to the Lord. We began to have lunch together and to read the Word and pray. What a difference her presence made in my days! Rather than dreading going to work, I would look forward to her insightful questions. When my supervisor made disparaging remarks about "Bible-thumping Christians," Bernice challenged me to walk my faith. Her hunger to learn led me to dig more deeply into God's Word.

I found that no matter how hard I tried to be positive and avoid gossip, it was almost impossible to accomplish alone. But with a friend it was easier. We could sit in the lunch room together and fashion our own conversations. The more we talked about the Lord, the more courageous we became. Then other people even began to join us. They would share a need or sometimes even ask for advice. Bernie and I tried to hold each other accountable to do the best job we could for the company. We helped each other remember not to visit on company time. We agreed not to "steal" from our employer by making personal phone calls or taking long breaks. She was as good an influence on me as I tried to be on her!

Today in my business, we encourage our employees to develop friendships with each other. We have become, in many ways, a family. In today's world, we often spend more hours each day with our work-mates than with our families at home. Close friendships at work can

*Friendships at work help us learn*

make us better people, and help us learn communication and problem-solving skills that can better our lives at home. Because my husband, Stephen, and I are Christians, we have provided a daily devotional break on company time. It is common to find our employees surrounding someone who is hurting and praying or counseling him or her. They also hold each other accountable to God's Word and his wisdom. They are involved in each other's lives, and it is one of our greatest joys to watch them help each other grow in the Lord and his wisdom. What a difference from my earlier work environment!

In life, all it takes is one person to help you become a better person or to drag you down. Be careful of the company you keep. Be careful of coarse jesting and negative conversations. Look for someone you can befriend and encourage in the Lord. God can use your workplace in amazing ways if you just ask him!

God is present in the company of the righteous

Psalms 14:5

# Lord,

Help me to make an impact in my workplace
and in daily life. Help me to be an example
of faith and faithfulness. Let me demonstrate
integrity, diligence, kindness, patience
and mercy.

Teach me to guard my speech carefully. . .
speaking only what you would say
if you were in my place.

It's so easy to be influenced negatively by those
around me, instead help me to be a godly
influence on those you've placed in my life.
And lead me to a friend or friends that will
encourage and challenge me to never forget
who you created me to be.

# *The man*

who plants and the man who waters
have one purpose, and each will be rewarded
according to his own labor.
For we are God's fellow workers;
you are God's field, God's building.
*1 Corinthians 3:8-9*

Let us not become weary in doing good,
for at the proper time we will reap a harvest
if we do not give up.
*Galatians 6:9*

Speaking the truth in love, we will in all things
grow up into him who is the Head, that is, Christ.
From him the whole body, joined and held together
by every supporting ligament, grows and builds
itself up in love, as each part does its work.
*Ephesians 4:15-16*

# The Best Friend Ever

Did you know that there is someone who longs to be your friend even more than I longed for Sally's friendship all those years ago? That someone is Jesus. His longing though, doesn't have anything to do with his neediness but is based on the profound and all-encompassing love he has for you.

In John 15:13-15 Jesus says, "Greater love has no one than this that he lay down his life for his friends. You are my friends if you do what I command. I no longer call you servants, because a servant does not know his master's business. Instead, I have called you friends, for everything that I learned from my Father I have made known to you." Jesus invites us to become his friends! Every aspect of friendship I have shared here and more

## "I have called you friends"

is also available between you and God. He wants to share intimately, heart-to-heart, with you. He wants to know about your daily concerns, needs, and desires. He hungers for you to share "the real you" with him, and he passionately desires to reveal himself to you as well.

Isn't that hard to imagine? The God who created the universe has the desire to spend time with you! God wants to be the kind of friend to you that will speak the truth in love, and yet be gracious enough not to tell you all of it at once! He wants to walk with you through the seasons of life, the times of joy and sorrow, the triumphs and heartaches. He wants to be your friend more than you can ever imagine or comprehend.

Try reading through these chapters again and allow God to show you how he wants this kind of relationship with you.

What is holding you back from that friendship? Do you feel unworthy? Do you feel like a failure? All you need to do is ask his forgiveness and he'll wipe your slate clean and give you a fresh new start. Is fear holding you back? Are you afraid that, like a hard taskmaster, he'll ask you to do things you cannot do, or that you'll never be able to "measure up" to his standards? His love for you is perfect; his will for your life is so far beyond what you can ever dream. When God does require a task of you, he will give you both the desire to do it and the skills to complete it.

*His love for you is perfect*

Imagine if the President of the United States said to you, "Will you be my friend? Will you come to the White House and walk in the rose garden and talk over the events of the day with me? Can I share my heart with you? Can I tell you the things I have planned?" If he provided the ticket, how long would it take you to pack and be there? How excited would you be?

God invites you...YOU... to his throne room. He gave you the ticket through the sacrifice of Jesus Christ on the cross. You couldn't have earned it. You surely don't deserve it. But still he invites you into his presence at any time, day or night, without an appointment. He's never in a hurry to get on to the next thing on his agenda. He has all the time in eternity to spend with you. No matter how needy you are, he won't get tired of helping you. There is no more faithful friend.

*There is no more faithful friend*

Will you accept his invitation to friendship? This simple prayer, or one from your own heart, is all it takes.

# Lord,

I can't imagine why you would want to be my friend. I'm a sinner, I constantly do what I know isn't right. The harder I try to be good, it seems, the bigger mess I make of things. Please forgive me. I want to be your child and your friend. Help me to become your friend. Give me the desire to obey your commandments. Give me the faith to believe in you, to trust in you, to love you and to freely come to your throne like a little child coming to sit on her father's lap—in freedom and without fear. Remove the places in my heart that have become damaged and fearful of intimacy and give me a new heart, one full of love for you. Thank you for the awesome invitation to become

# Your Friend.

# God

demonstrates his own love for us in this:
While we were still sinners, Christ died for us.
*Romans 5:8*

The LORD your God is with you,
he is mighty to save. He will take great delight in you,
he will quiet you with his love, he will
rejoice over you with singing.
*Zephaniah 3:17*

Cast all your anxiety on God
because he cares for you.
*1 Peter 5:7*

Jesus said, "Here I am! I stand at the door and knock.
If anyone hears my voice and opens the door,
I will come in and eat with him and he with me."
*Revelation 3:20*